A
Patchwork
of
Blessings & Graces

A
Patchwork
of
Blessings & Graces

Edited by Mary Daniels

First published in 1996 jointly by

Gracewing		Peake Road
Fowler Wright Books	&	6316 Peake Road
Southern Avenue		Macon
Leominster		Georgia 31210-3960
Herefordshire HR6 0Q		USA

Peake Road is an imprint of Smyth & Helwys Publishing, Inc®

UK ISBN 0 85244 323 4   US ISBN 1 57312 050 2

Typesetting by
Action Typesetting Ltd, Gloucester, GL1 1SP

Printed by
Cromwell Press, Broughton Gifford, Wiltshire, SN12 8PH

Contents

Author's Note   vii
Meal time Graces   1
Topical Graces   11
Local Graces   41
Quiet time Graces   53
Personal Graces   63
Subject Index   76
Authors Index   77

Author's Note

A Patchwork of Blessings and Graces

Blessings and Graces are like snowflakes. They drift, change and hover silently and without weight. Although they may look similar, each one is slightly different. They come when least expected, but when they do arrive their impact can be breathtaking.

My collection has been gathered from many sources. As so many are traditional or passed by word of mouth it is not possible to acknowledge them all. Many are attributed to several authors. Some have travelled through the mists of time. Passing on a blessing is like playing the whispering game. We do not always hear the same words, but it is the giving and sharing of the message that matters.

I have been a word squirrel for many years and have tucked away trivia, prayers, quotations, poems and kind words into a storehouse of treasures. They have come from monuments, menus, church notice sheets, fusty second-hand books, glossy magazines, posters, after show suppers, formal dinners and humble feasts. In fact, a blessing can be found hidden in the most surprising places; forgiveness in a concentration camp; gratitude when hungry; praise when life is at its lowest ebb.

Some of the items are original and many come from the social lives of friends and colleagues. More unusual sources are a Cornish chapel half hidden in the rocks and the bathroom wall of a nunnery.

History and literature have produced some wonderful and poignant calls to God for help not only to bless meal times but to take sides in conflicts. The prayer of Shakespeare's Henry V:

O God of battles, steel my soldiers' hearts,
Possess them not with fear. Take from them now
The sense of reckoning,

was a powerful and poetic grace before war – in complete contrast to the simple request of the evangelist Billy Graham:

May the Lord bless you real good.

In the early days of the Church, a plague broke out in Rome, of which the first symptom was a sneeze. To this day, even people who would never dream of asking for a blessing at meal-times, still say 'Bless You' for every sneeze. That gentle snowflake, which originally stemmed from fear, has refused to melt after centuries of use.

Many people have asked me to supply them with a grace for a particular function. It is hard to find the exact words for each occasion, but it is vital to do one's best to match the words to the event as the wrong impression can hurt and do more harm than good. George Eliot, the nineteenth century English author, whose real name was Mary Ann Evans, once wrote:

> Blessed is the man who, having nothing to say, abstains from giving in words evidence of the fact.

Clearly she realised how important it is to say the right thing at the right time.

The word 'Grace' comes from the Latin 'Gratia' meaning pleasantness or charm. This anthology could almost be described as a bouquet of charm, as the literal transation of the word 'Anthology' is 'A collection of flowers', from the Greek words 'Anthus' meaning flower and 'Logos' meaning word.

Bishop Cyril of Jerusalem (c. 315 – 386 AD) understood this connection between grace and nature. 'Why did Christ refer to Grace of the Spirit under the name of water? Because the water of rain comes down from Heaven, and though rain comes down in one form its effects take many forms. Yea, one spring watered Paradise, and the same rain falls on the whole world, yet it becomes white in the lily, red in the rose, purple in the violet.'

In the Bible, after God had created Adam and Eve, 'He blessed them'. They did not ask for a blessing. It was a gift, God's first blessing to man.

Now, when we say a grace before eating, it is done more out of courtesy, praise and thanks to Him who made the basic ingredients which enable our survival and pleasure. Yet in areas of the world where there is famine, it can be a matter of life and death. That is why many of the graces chosen include a call to remember those less fortunate than ourselves.

We all remember the joke about the little girl who was told to eat up her rice pudding and remember the starving. 'Well, give it to them,' she replied. These days, with proliferating charities and easier world communication it should not be necessary to have to pray for the starving, but unfortunately it is. Rice should be accessible to all – but unfortunately it is not.

Who knows how one little grace can help even one person in some small way, just as no snowscape could exist without each tiny particle of snow.

If your snowflake has drifted into my book, please accept my thanks and gratitude. If it is not acknowledged, forgive me – and in the words of one of the earliest and most long-lasting blessings of all time, from the Book of Numbers:

May the Lord bless you and keep you.
May the Lord let His face shine on you and be gracious to you.
May the Lord uncover His face to you and bring you peace.

Meal time Graces

Our Daily Bread

For what we are about to receive, May the
    Lord make us truly thankful

Anon

We are what we eat

Anon

The Lord showers us with blessings,
They fall in many places.
Please forgive the words I've caught
Without the names and faces.

Anon

Old English Prayer

Give us Lord, a bit o' sun,
A bit o' work, a bit o' fun,
Give us in all the struggle and sputter;
Our daily bread and a bit o' butter.
Give us health our keep to make
And a bit to spare for other's sake.
Give us, too, a bit of song,
And a tale and a book to help us along.
Give us Lord, a chance to be
Our goodly best, brave, wise and free,
Our goodly best, for ourselves and others
Till all men learn to live as brothers.

Xmas Anon

For food, friends and fellowship may we be
always thankful

Anon

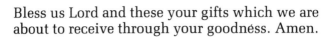

Bless us Lord and these your gifts which we are
about to receive through your goodness. Amen.

Anon

May this food and wine,
Our joy and pleasure,
Help us to give
In equal measure.

Anon

May our God be with us as we share Earth's
fruitfulness, and may those who have nothing
be allowed their share of it also.

Anon

Lord, give us strength to take what comes
With deep contentment,
Remembering those who have no dinner,
And what we ought to give
To relieve their plight.

Anon

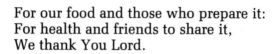

For our food and those who prepare it:
For health and friends to share it,
We thank You Lord.

Anon

Remind us Lord that as we receive, so should we
give, that we may all enjoy the gifts of an
abundant Earth.

Anon

For food and health and hope, we thank you
Lord.
Give us a generous hand to share these gifts with
others.

Anon

Welcome Lord, come Lord be our guest,
And may our meal by you be blessed.

Anon

God of Goodness, bless our food.
Keep us in a pleasant mood.
Bless the cook and all who serve us,
From indigestion, Lord, preserve us.

Anon

―――――

For the Meal,
For every joy,
We praise you, Lord.

Anon

―――――

Eat well and drink well,
And serve God devoutly.

Grace of St Hugh of Lincoln (1140 – 1200), who was born in Burgundy. He was called to England by Henry II to be Abbot of a Carthusian monastery founded by the King as part of his penance after ordering the death of St Thomas á Becket.

A Prayer for Good Digestion

Give me a good digestion, Lord.
And also something to digest:
Give me a healthy body, Lord,
With sense to keep it at its best.

Give me a healthy mind, good Lord,
To keep the good and pure in sight,
Which seeing sin is not appalled
But finds a way to set it right;
Give me a mind that is not bored,
That does not whimper, whine or sigh:
Don't let me worry overmuch
About the fussy thing called I.

Give me a sense of humour, Lord,
Give me the grace to see a joke,
To get some happiness in life
And pass it on to other folk.

Found in Chester Cathedral   *Anon*

The Loaves and Fishes

Christ in the wilderness – five thousand fed:
Two small fishes and five loaves of bread.
May the blessing of Him
Who made the division,
Rest upon us
And upon our provision.

Anon

O Lord, who made these loaves and fishes,
Look down upon these two poor dishes
And, though they be exceeding small,
Make them enough, we pray, for all;
For if they should our stomachs fill,
Heaven will have wrought a miracle.

Anon

Traditional Graces

Bless, O Lord, this food to our use,
And us to Thy service,
And make us ever mindful
Of the needs of others.

Anon

———————

God give us work until our lives end,
And life until our work is done.

Anon

Topical Graces

For World Hunger

For food in a world where many walk in
   hunger;
For faith in a world where many walk in fear;
For friends in a world where many walk alone;
We give you humble thanks, O Lord.

The Girl Guide Grace

In a somewhere hungry, sometimes lonely
world, for this food and this fellowship may we
be truly thankful. Amen.

Anon

A Prayer for Those who Suffer

O merciful Father,
by your word and Holy Spirit
comfort all who are suffering or in distress.
Turn their hearts to you,
that they may serve you in truth,
and bear fruit to your glory.
help and protect them, O Lord;
through Jesus Christ our Lord.
Amen.

Philip Melanchthon (1497 – 1560),
German Reformer

A Mother's Grace

God created corn and grapes
That human hands have tended.
Please God bless our bread and wine;
And when our meal is ended,
Bless our minds and guide our way
To help those who have starved today.

Mary Daniels

Mothers' Day Prayer

We pray you Lord to listen
To every mother's prayer.
We ask you for your blessing
On mothers everywhere.

Anon

Two Graces for Children

Bless us O God as we sit together.
Bless the food we eat today.
Bless the hands that made the food.
Bless us O God.
Amen.

Anon

May God bless all children, everywhere, especially those at risk in the world. May God bless all those whose job it is to bring light, laughter and happiness to others. May God bless the good fellowship of this table, and may we never fail those in need.

The Very Reverend Peter Berry,
Provost of St Philip's Cathedral, Birmingham

Childrens Graces

Praise to the God who giveth meat
Convenient unto all who eat:
Praise for tea and buttered toast,
Father, Son and Holy Ghost.

R. L. Gales

For every cup and plateful
Lord, make us truly grateful.

A. S. T. Fisher

A Child's Prayer

Through the night Thy angels kept
Watch above me while I slept,
Now the dark has passed away,
Thank Thee, Lord, for this new day.

North and south and east and west
May Thy holy name be blest:
Everywhere beneath the sun,
As in Heaven Thy will be done.

Give me food that I may live;
Every naughtiness forgive:
Keep all evil things away
From Thy little child this day.

William Canton

A Blessing for All Children

May God bless the world's children and keep
them safe:
May God bless all children in cities and those
who care for them:
May God bless the good and fellowship of this
evening, and give us generous hearts.
Amen.

The Very Reverend Peter Berry,
Provost of St Philip's Cathedral, Birmingham

For Parents and All Who Care for Children

If a child lives with criticism, he learns to condemn.
If a child lives with hostility, he learns to fight.
If a child lives with ridicule, he learns to feel guilty.
If a child lives with unfairness, he learns to mistrust.

But . . .

If a child lives with tolerance, he learns to be patient.
If a child lives with encouragement, he gains confidence.
If a child lives with approval, he will appreciate others.
If a child lives with fair discipline, he will learn justice.
If a child lives with security, he will discover faith.
If a child lives with kindness, he will be kind to others.

Lord, may all adults learn to be tolerant, fair and kind, and to give encouragement, love and security to children everywhere.

Anon

Grace for the Fight

Oh Lord, Thou knowest how busy I must be today; If I forget Thee, do not Thou forget me.

Sir Jacob Astley's plea before going into battle for the King's troops at the Battle of Naseby June 14 1645.

Lord Nelson's Grace

God save the Queen,
Bless our dinners,
Make us thankful.
Amen.

Blessing of the Cheese and Olives

Sanctify this milk that has been pressed into cheese, and press us together in charity. Grant that this fruit of the olive-tree may never lose its savour; for the olive is a symbol of that abundance which, at your bidding, flowered from the tree and is there for those who trust you.

A second-century grace

A Grace for Seamen

Let us give thanks for safety from the sea,
And for this bread with these our gathered friends.

Response to be said by all present:

May the Light guide us till our sailing ends.

John Masefield (1878 – 1966)

Grace written for
Queen Elizabeth I in 1565

God bless our meat,
God guide our ways,
God give us grace
Our Lord to please.
Lord, long preserve in peace and health
Our gracious Queen Elizabeth.

George Bellin

A Grace for Christmas Day

Reflect upon your present blessings, of which every man has many; not upon your past misfortunes, of which all men have some.

Charles Dickens, from Sketches by Boz

Blessing for a Wartime Tea

Upon a scanty meal, O Lord,
Bestow a blessing in accord:
Pour Thy grace in measure small,
Lest it more than cover all.

Bless the tiny piece of ham:
Bless the lonely dab of jam:
Bless the sparsely-buttered toast,
Father, Son and Holy Ghost.

Allan Laing

A Traditional Nursery Rhyme

There was once a goose and a wren
Who gave lunch to a cock and a hen:
'O Lord' prayed the goose,
'Bless these gifts to our use
And ourselves in Thy service.
Amen.'

Anon

A Grace to a Haggis

Fair Fa' your honest soncie face,
Great chieftain of the puddin' race!
Aboon them a' ye tak your place,
Painch, tripe, or thairm:
Weel are ye worthy o' a grace
As lang's my arm.

Robert Burns (1769 – 1796)

A Friendship Grace

For our food before us,
Our Friends beside us,
And our Fellowship around the world,
We thank you Lord.

Anon

A New Testament Grace

Grace be unto you, and peace, from him which
is, and which was, and which is to come.

Revelation of Saint John 1:4

A Courteous Grace

Of courtesy – it is much less
Than courage of heart or holiness;
Yet in my walks it seems to me
That the grace of God is in courtesy.

Hilaire Belloc (1870 – 1953)

A Grace for a Club or Association

Lord, We pray for all people living in areas of
great distress.
We hope that, through our Association, we can
help them in some way.
We count our blessings that we live in peace.
Amen.

Barbara Marshall

A Prayer Book Grace

Grant that those things we ask faithfully we
may obtain effectually.

The Book of Common Prayer, 1662

A Grace for The Home

Plenty of Grace
Be to this Place.

Cartouche on a Tudor Manor House in Somerset

♥ ♥ ♥ ♥ ♥ ♥ ♥ ♥ ♥ ♥ ♥

A Prayer for Life

Life is a challenge . . . meet it;
Life is a gift . . . accept it;
Life is a sorrow . . . overcome it;
Life is a tragedy . . . face it;
Life is a duty . . . perform it;
Life is a game . . . play it;
Life is a mystery . . . unfold it;
Life is a song . . . sing it;
Life is an opportunity . . . take it;
Life is a journey . . . complete it;
Life is a promise . . . fulfill it;
Life is a beauty . . . praise it;
Life is a struggle . . . fight it;
Life is a goal . . . achieve it;
Life is a puzzle . . . solve it;
Life is love . . . love it.

Found on the bathroom wall of a
Retreat House

♥ ♥ ♥ ♥ ♥ ♥ ♥ ♥ ♥ ♥ ♥ ♥

Graces for Struggling Weightwatchers

Hearken diligently to Me, and eat what is good and delight yourselves in fatness.

Isaiah 55:2

───────

Eat drink and be merry, for tomorrow ye diet.

Lewis C. Henry

───────

A Proud Person's Grace

Lord, help us to see that swallowing our pride is non-fattening; that sweet words are easier to eat than thoughtless ones and that forbidden fruit makes bad jam.

Anon

Hot Weather Prayer

For water ices, cheap but good,
That find us in a thirsty mood;
For ices made of milk or cream
That slip down smoothly as a dream;
For cornets, sandwiches and pies,
That make the gastric juices rise;
For ices bought in little shops
Or at the kerb from him who stops;
For chanting of the sweet refrain:
'Vanilla, strawberry or plain?'
We thank Thee Lord, who sendst with heat
This cool deliciousness to eat.

Allan Laing

Oops!

Dear Lord, please put Your arm round my shoulder and Your hand over my mouth.

The prayer of an anonymous American Lady

─────

A missionary translating his favourite blessing into an African dialect transformed it from, 'Lord, dismiss us with Thy blessing' into 'Lord, kick us out softly.'

Anon

─────

A German priest working in Birmingham decided to change his usual blessing of 'May the Lord preserve you'. After looking through the dictionary, he proudly beamed from the pulpit, 'May the Lord pickle you.'

Anon

The Round Table Grace

May we, O Lord, adopt Thy creed,
Adapt our ways to serve They need,
And we, who on Thy bounty feed,
Improve in thought, and word, and
   deed.

Anon

The Rotarian Grace

We bless thee Lord, for this our food,
For life and health and every good.
May we more blest than we deserve
Live less for self and more to serve.

Anon

The Inner Wheel Grace

For the food that you give
For the fellowship we share
For the friendship we cherish
We thank you for your care.
Amen

Bridget Lewis

A Quaker Prayer

O God, help us not to despise or oppose what
we do not understand.
Amen.

William Penn (1644 – 1718),
English Quaker, founder of Pennsylvania

A Quaker Grace

Us and this: God bless.

Anon

A Motorist's Prayer

Lord, grant me a steady hand and a watchful
  eye,
That no man may be hurt when I pass by.
Thou givest life; I pray no act of mine
May take away, or mar this act of Thine.
Save those, dear Lord, who bear me company,
From shock and pain and all calamity.
Teach me to use my car for others' need
And not to miss, through simple love of speed
The beauty of this world, that so I may
With joy and courtesy go on my way.

Anon

―――――

A Farmer's Grace

At Christmas play and make good cheer,
For Christmas comes but once a year.

Thomas Tusser (1515 – 1580),
from The Farmer's Daily Diet

A Sinner's Grace

May we who are sinners
Deserve our dinners.

Rabbi Lionel Blue's favourite grace

A Golfer's Grace

Whether the day has been one of under or over par, let us share and enjoy, in each other's company, the relaxations of the nineteenth green.
We ask the Lord's blessing on the meal we are about to have, and on all those who have worked to tee up the day and evening.
We also ask the Lord's blessing on ourselves. Amen.

The Reverend Ray Zacaroli

A Fisherman's Prayer

Give me, O Lord, to catch a fish
So large that even I,
In boasting of it afterwards,
Shall have no need to lie.

Anon

♥ ♥ ♥ ♥ ♥ ♥ ♥ ♥ ♥ ♥ ♥ ♥

A Sparrow's Prayer

Father, before this sparrow's earthly flight
Ends in the darkness of a winter's night;
Father, without whose word no sparrow falls,
Hear this, thy weary sparrow, when he calls.
Mercy, not justice, is his contrite prayer,
Cancel his guilt, and drive away despair;
Speak but the word, and make his spirit
   whole,
Cleanse the dark places of his heart and soul.
Speak but the word, and set his spirit free;
Mercy, not justice, still his constant plea,
So shall the sparrow, crumpled wings
   restored,
Soar like the lark, and glorify his Lord.

from Lord Hailsham's memoirs, The Sparrow's
Flight

A Poet's Graces

What God gives, and what we take,
'Tis the gift for Christ His sake:
Be the meal of beans or peas,
God be thanked for those, and these:
Have we flesh, or have we fish,
All are fragments from His dish.
He His church save, and the King,
And our peace here, like the Spring,
Make it ever flourishing.

Robert Herrick (1591 – 1674),
poet and clergyman

Here a little child I stand
Heaving up my either hand;
Cold as paddocks though they be,
Here I lift them up to Thee,
For a Benison to fall
On our meat, and on us all.
Amen.

Robert Herrick, from Paddocks are toads

Some hae meat and canna eat,
And some would eat that want it;
But we hae meat, and we can eat,
Sae let the Lord be thankit.

Grace before meat, Robert Burns,

Local Graces

A Welsh Grace

Let us be thankful for whatever light, laughter, food and affection may come our way.
And let us be mindful equally of those who at this time or some future moment may be sadly without any or all of these good and golden things.

Grace of Gwyn Thomas, novelist

Cornish Grace

Dew ollgallosek, merasta – Why!
Amen.

Almighty God, much thanks to You, Amen.
Anon

An Old Irish Grace

May the blessing of the loaves and fishes which
Our Lord shared among the multitude, and the
grace from the King who made the sharing, be
upon us and our partaking.
Amen

Anon

Old Scottish Grace

Lord, grant that we may always be right, for
Thou knowest we are hard to turn.

Anon

A Hebrew Grace

Blessed be Thou, Lord God of the Universe, who bringest forth bread from the earth and makest glad the hearts of men.

Anon

A Hebrew Warning

He who eats and drinks, but does not bless the Lord, is a thief.

Anon

Graces from Poland

Before Meals:

Bless, O Lord, us and these gifts of yours which
we shall eat, thanks to your munificence.

Anon

After Meals:

We thank you, O omnipotent God, for all your
kindnesses. You, who live and reign for ever
and ever.
Amen.

Anon

♥ ♥ ♥ ♥ ♥ ♥ ♥ ♥ ♥ ♥ ♥ ♥

A Chinese Prayer

Lord, revive your church, beginning with me.

Anon

―――――

Prayer from an African Child

Oh Thou great chief, light a candle in my heart, that I may see what is therein and sweep the rubbish from Thy dwelling place.

Anon

Some American Graces

Lord, give us faith that right makes might.

Abraham Lincoln (1809 – 1865)

―――――

God bless all those that I love.
God bless all those that love me.
God bless all those that love those that I love
And all those that love those that love me.

*From a seventeenth-century New England
sampler*

―――――

America! America!
God shed his Grace on thee
And crown thy good with brotherhood
From sea to shining sea!

*From America the Beautiful by
Katherine Lee Bates (1859 – 1929)*

I, when I undress me,
Each night upon my knees,
Will pray the Lord to bless me
With apple pie and cheese.

Anon

———————————

The Lord is good to me,
And so I thank the Lord
For giving me the things I need,
The sun, the rain, the appleseed.
The Lord is good to me.

And every seed that grows,
Will grow into a tree.
And one day soon
There'll be apples there,
For everyone in the world to share,
The Lord is good to me.

Grace by American pioneer,
John Chapman (1774 – 1845)

A British Prayer

Lord God, we thank you for all your gifts in the abundance of your creation, and in the service of our lives.
We pray for our Queen and our Commonwealth and for the integrity of the Realm.

As we gather at this table, help us to remember those in need: in our own city, and far around the world.

May we eat and drink in charity and under-standing, and receive the spiritual food of your all-sustaining goodness.
Through Jesus Christ Our Lord.
Amen

The Very Reverend Peter Berry
Provost of St Philip's Cathedral, Birmingham

A Prayer for the Australian Outback

Bare feet are better;
the humility to learn
the desert's ways,
its secret life,
its hidden water.

The Lord of the prophets is near:
'I am who I am'.
Moses and Elijah,
the Baptist, and Jesus
grew tall here.

From Outback Reflections *by Bruce Prewer*

Quiet time Graces

Time for Grace

Time is ... Too slow for those who wait
Too swift for those who fear
Too long for those who grieve
Too short for those who rejoice
But for those who love
Time is eternity.
Lord give us the grace and time to love and care.

Anon

Bite off more than you can chew ... then
   chew it.
Plan for more than you can do ... then do it.
Point your arrow to a star,
Take your aim from where you are.
Arrange more time than you can spare ...
   then spare it.
Take on more than you can bear ... then bear
   it.
Plan your castle in the air,
Then build a ship to take you there
Lord, help us all to do our share.

Anon

A Sabbath Prayer

May the Lord protect and defend you,
May He always shield you from shame;
May you come to be
In Israel a shining name;
May you be like Ruth and like Esther,
May you be deserving of praise;
Strengthen them, O Lord
And keep them from the stranger's ways.

May God bless you
And grant you long lives.

May the Lord fulfill our Sabbath prayer for you,
May God make you
Good mothers and wives,
May He send you husbands who will care for
   you,
May the Lord protect and defend you.

May the Lord preserve you from pain.
Favour them O Lord
With happiness and peace,
O hear our Sabbath prayer.
Amen.

From Fiddler on the Roof

♥ ♥ ♥ ♥ ♥ ♥ ♥ ♥ ♥ ♥ ♥ ♥

A Shaker Prayer

Wherever the power of God is felt or perceived, there is the God of Power.... Where the spirit of God is, there is God, for God is spirit ... Happy are they who heartily and habitually believe in the Omnipresence and infinite goodness of God, the Heavenly Father and Mother, and who are reconciled to everything which He permits; who see his footsteps in every thing without them, and feel Him 'working within them to will and to do of his own good pleasure,' being conscious that they are daily and faithful co-workers with him.

The Shaker, I, 11, pp. 86 – 87, 1871

O Lord Remember

O Lord remember . . .
Not only the men and women of good will,
but also those of ill will.
But do not only remember all the suffering
they have inflicted on us,
remember the fruits we brought, thanks to this
   suffering,
our comradeship, our loyalty, our humility,
the courage, the generosity,
the greatness of heart which has grown out of
   all this,
and when they come to judgement,
let all the fruits that we have borne
be their forgiveness.

*Prayer found on a piece of wrapping paper near the
body of a dead child in Ravensbruck, a Nazi
Concentration Camp where 92,000 women and
children died in World War II.*

God be in my Head

God by in my head,
And in my understanding;

God be in mine eyes,
And in my looking;

God be in my mouth,
And in my speaking;

God be in my heart,
And in my thinking.

God be at mine end,
And at my departing.

The Primer

A Pilgrim's Blessing

May the Babe of Bethlehem be yours to tend;
May the Boy of Nazareth be yours for friend;
May the Man of Galilee His healing send;
May the Christ of Calvary His courage lend;
May the Risen Lord His presence send;
And His holy angels defend you to the end.

from Oberammergau, Germany

Personal Graces

Personal Graces

O Word of Waters
Be born on my lips
So may I be Thy word.

O Gift of Fire
Be born in my heart
So may I be Thy gift.

O Bread of Earth
Be born in my hands
So may I be Thy food.

Leo Baker

────────────

For food and fellowship
And all the love and beauty
And bounty of Heaven and Earth
We give Thee thanks.

Will Sawkins

For the words which feed our minds;
For the food which feeds our bodies;
For the love which feeds our love for you and
our neighbour,
We thank you Lord.

John Daniels

O Lord,
never let us think that we can stand by
ourselves, and not need you.
Amen.

John Donne (1572 – 1631),
English poet and preacher

O God, grant us serenity to accept what cannot
be changed, the courage to change what can be
changed, and the wisdom to know the
difference.

Reinhold Niebuhr (1892 – 1971),
American theologian

Lord God,
of your goodness give me yourself, for you are
enough for me, and only in you have I all.
Amen.

The Lady Julian of Norwich (c. 1342 – c. 1413),
mystic and anchoress

An Archbishop's Grace

Lord our God, give us grace to desire you with a
whole heart,
that so desiring we may seek and find you,
and so finding may love you,
and loving you may hate those sins which
separate us from you;
for the sake of Jesus Christ.
Amen.

Saint Anselm (1033 – 1109),
sometime Archbishop of Canterbury

———

A Bishop's Grace

Lord, forgive us that we feast while others
  starve.

The Grace of Bishop Charles Gore (1853 – 1932)
sometime Bishop of Birmingham

Gemma's Graces

For the Harvest Festival:

Thank you Jesus,
For the fishermen who work all day.
Thank you for the farmers
Who grow wheat for our cereals
And corn for our flour and bread;
For the vineyard owners,
Who grow grapes for our wine.
Thank you for our milk and cream;
For our cheese and lollies;
Thank you for our apples, lemons,
Oranges, pears and our potatoes
And beans, carrots
And lots of other vegetables;
For our salads like peppers,
Lettuces, tomatoes and cucumbers,
But most of all, thank you for
The rain and the sun,
That makes the harvest grow for everyone.
Amen

This day you gave us Lord
Will never come again.
Tomorrow has still yet to come
Yesterday has been and gone
But still your love goes on and on.

―――――――

Gemma's Goodnight

When my mother tucks me up,
When I snuggle down in bed;
When my father says, 'Sleep tight,'
When the moon shines nice and bright,
All the stars sparkle
And say, 'Good Night.'

Gemma Vandome, aged nine

Two Pauline Graces

Let your speech be always with grace, seasoned with salt.

From Saint Paul's Letter to the Colossians

By the Grace of God, I am what I am.

From Saint Paul's First Letter to the Corinthians

Two Graces by
Dean Jonathan Swift

For rabbits young and rabbits old,
For rabbits hot and rabbits cold,
For rabbits tender and rabbits tough,
We thank Thee Lord: we've had enough.

———

Does any man of common sense
Think ham and eggs give God offence?
Or that a herring has a charm
The Almighty's anger to disarm?
Wrapped in His Majesty divine
D'you think He cares on what we dine?

Composed, it is said, when given bacon and eggs for breakfast in an Irish monastery, when all the monks were eating fish because it was Friday.

Jonathan Swift (1667 – 1745) sometime Dean of Saint Patrick's Cathedral, Dublin

Prayer of Saint Francis of Assisi

Lord, make me an instrument of Thy peace;
Where there is hate that I may bring love,
Where there is offence that I may bring
   pardon,
Where there is discord that I may bring union,
Where there is error that I may bring truth,
Where there is doubt that I may bring faith,
Where there is despair that I may bring hope,
Where there is darkness that I may bring light,
Where there is sadness that I may bring joy,
O Master, make me not so much to be
   consoled as to console;
Not so much to be loved as to love;
Not so much to be understood as to
   understand;
For it is in giving that one receives;
It is in self-forgetfulness that one finds;
It is in pardoning that one is pardoned;
It is in dying that one finds eternal life.

Saint Francis of Assisi (1182 – 1226),
Founder of the Franciscan Order

A Morning Thanksgiving

Thank God for sleep in the long quiet night,
For the clear day calling through the little
    leaded panes,
For the shining well-water and the warm
    golden light,
And the paths washed white by singing rains.

We thank Thee, O God, for exultation born
Of the kiss of Thy winds, for life among the
    leaves,
For the whirring wings that pass about the
    wonder of the morn
For the changing plumes of swallows gliding
    upwards in their eaves.

For the treasures of the garden, the
    gillyflowers of gold,
The prouder petalled tulips, the primrose full
    of spring,
For the crowded orchard boughs, and the
    swelling buds that hold
A yet unwoven wonder, to Thee our praise we
    bring.

Thank God for good bread, for the honey in
the comb,
For the brown-shelled eggs, for the clustered
blossoms set
Beyond the open window in a pink and
cloudy foam,
For the laughing doves among the branches
met.

For the kindly-faced women we bring our
thanks to Thee,
With shapely mothering arms and grave eyes
clear and blithe,
For the tall young men, strong-thewed as men
may be,
For the old man bent above his scythe.

For earth's little secret and innumerable ways,
For the carol and the colour, Lord we bring
What things may be of thanks, and that Thou
hast lent our days,
Eyes to see and ears to hear and lips to sing.

John Drinkwater

A Last Thought

'God bless us everyone!' said Tiny Tim.

from A Christmas Carol *by Charles Dickens*

Subject Index

America 48, 49
Australia 51
Bishops 67
Britain 50
Birds 37
Bread 65
Children 15, 16, 17, 18, 19, 47
Chinese 47
Christmas Day 22
Clubs 26
Contentment 5
Cornish 43
Courtesy 26
Farmers 34
Fisherman 36
Friends 6, 25
Fruitfulness 5
Girl Guides 13
Golfers 35
Good Digestion 8
Haggis 24
Harvest Festival 68
Health 6
Hebrew 45
Her Majesty the Queen 20
Home 27
Hot Weather 30

Humour 8
Hunger 13
Inner Wheel 33
Irish 44
Life 28
Loves & Fishes 9
Mothers 14, 15
Motorists 34
New Testament 25
Nursery Rhyme 23
Olives 21
Pilgrims 61
Poets 38
Poland 46
Pride 29
Quakers 33
Rotary 32
Round Table 32
Sabbath 57
Scottish 44
Seamen 21
Serenity 66
Shakers 58
Sinners 35
Suffering 14
Thanksgiving 73
Weightwatchers 29
Welsh 43

Author Index

Anselm, Saint 67
Astley, Sir Jacob 20
Baker, Leo 65
Bates, Katherine Lee 48
Bellin, George 22
Belloc, Hilaire 26
Berry, Very Revd Peter 16, 18, 50
Blue, Rabbi Lionel 35
Burns, Robert 24, 39
Canton, William 17
Chapman, John 49
Daniels, John 66
Daniels, Mary 14
Dickens, Charles 22, 75
Donne, John 66
Drinkwater, John 74
Fisher, A S T 16
Francis of Assisi, Saint 72
Gales, R L 16
Gore, Bishop Charles 67
Hailsham, Lord 37
Henry, Lewis C 29

Herrick, Robert 38
Hugh of Lincoln, St 7
John the Divine, St 25
Laing, Allan 23; 30
Lewis, Bridget 33
Lincoln, Abraham 48
Marshall, Barbara 26
Masefield, John 21
Melancthon, Philip 14
Nelson, Admiral Lord Horatio 20
Niebuhr, Reinhold 66
Norwich, Lady Julian of 66
Paul, Saint 70
Penn, William 33
Prewer, Bruce 51
Sawkins, Will 65
Swift, Dean Jonathan 71
Thomas, Gwyn 43
Tusser, Thomas 34
Vandome, Gemma 68, 69
Zacaroli, Revd Ray 35